DISCOVER
Your Career

Careers If You Like
Working with People

Carla Mooney

ReferencePoint Press

San Diego, CA

ReferencePoint Press®

Printed in the United States

For more information, contact:
ReferencePoint Press, Inc.
PO Box 27779
San Diego, CA 92198
www.ReferencePointPress.com

LIBRARY OF CONGRESS CATALOGING-IN-PUBLICATION DATA

Author: Carla Mooney
Title: Careers If You Like Working with People
Description: San Diego, CA : ReferencePoint Press, 2026.
Series: Discover Your Career
Includes bibliographical references and index
Identifiers: LCCN 2025038671 (print) | ISBN 9781678212247 library binding | ISBN 9781678212254 ebook

For compete cataloging-in-publication data please go to www.loc.gov.

Contents

Introduction: Why People Skills Matter

When Drew Dudek was sixteen years old, he dreamed of playing college basketball. He was just starting his junior year of high school and expected to be a starter on his school's varsity basketball team. To stay in shape for basketball, Dudek ran cross-country track in the fall. But during one race, Dudek felt something pop in his right lower leg. At first, he thought the injury was minor and just needed a little rest to recover. When he still could not run after two weeks, Dudek went to the doctor for a magnetic resonance imaging scan. The scan revealed a large stress fracture in his lower leg bone, the tibia. Dudek was devastated to learn the injury would cause him to miss at least half of the upcoming basketball season.

As part of his recovery plan, Dudek began working with a physical therapist (PT). Dudek says:

> Luckily for me, my PT played college basketball, so we had an instant connection, and I listened to him even though I didn't want to. He was able to somehow turn my negative attitude into a positive one in the blink of an eye. It was almost like a switch went off when he explained to me that the goal wasn't to just get me back to playing basketball, but to get me back stronger than ever before. Something as simple as showing me that I was in his best interest made me trust him and have a positive outlook on PT. How powerful is that?[1]

The experience had an impact on Dudek. "From that day forward, I knew I wanted to be a PT. I wanted to impact people's lives in the same way that my PT changed mine. I wanted to be able to help people return to doing things that they love to do in the same way that he did for me,"[2] says Dudek.

Today Dudek has a doctorate in physical therapy and is a certified athletic trainer. He works daily with patients, especially athletes, helping them recover from injuries. "The impact we have on people's lives is what makes this profession so great. I'll never forget the look on my first patient's face when he came in for his final visit and told me that he was now able to perform his daily walking without any issues. He was as happy as can be, but little did he know that I was more excited than he was. I think it is safe to say that I made the right choice,"[3] Dudek says.

A People-Centered Career

When exploring future careers, people should consider their interests and the activities they enjoy. Some people naturally like talking, helping others, and working as part of a team. They might feel energized by group activities or simply enjoy making someone's day better. These individuals are often called "people persons" and thrive on human connection.

Often, people who enjoy working with others have strong communication, social, and interpersonal skills. In many careers, these skills are in high demand, whether working in a team, solving problems with others, or providing excellent service. These people skills help build trust, strengthen relationships, encourage collaboration, and generally make everyone feel comfortable.

People-centered careers exist in nearly every industry, from health care and education to hospitality, public service, and the arts. There are many benefits to working with people. It can be deeply rewarding to make a difference in someone's life, whether by offering support, solving a problem, or simply being a kind and helpful presence. Teamwork and good communication also lead to better outcomes and a more positive work environment. For those who enjoy working with others, there are countless career paths in which social and communication skills are in demand. Having such skills can help anyone build a successful and rewarding career.

Event Planner

What Does an Event Planner Do?

Planning events, from a wedding with two hundred guests to a convention with thousands of attendees, is the job of an event planner. Event planners oversee a wide range of events, including weddings, business meetings, fundraisers, and conferences. They make sure every detail of the event is perfect, from selecting a location to choosing the menu.

> **At a Glance**
>
> **Number of Jobs**
> 149,000 in 2023
>
> **Pay**
> $59,440 median pay in 2024
>
> **Educational Requirements**
> Bachelor's degree
>
> **Personal Qualities**
> Good communicator, interpersonal skills, organizational skills, problem-solving skills
>
> **Working Conditions**
> Offices, hotels, conference centers
>
> **Future Job Outlook**
> Growth of 7 percent through 2033

Planning an event of any size starts with a client meeting. Event planners talk with clients to gather information about an event, its purpose, and objectives. For example, a business meeting for top-performing sales employees will have different needs than a public convention for comic book fans. Event planners work with clients to estimate the number of attendees and develop a vision for the event. They also set the event's budget with clients.

Armed with this information, event planners research and visit potential event locations, such as hotels, parks, restaurants, and convention centers. They consider the location's characteristics and determine whether it meets the client's needs. Once they have found the right location, event planners book the space. Then they work with staff at the venue and outside vendors to plan details such as food, tables, decorations, technology, entertainment, and special activities. Event planners also collaborate with local vendors and hotels to arrange accommodations, transportation, and other essential needs for attendees.

During events, event planners are typically on-site, ensuring that everything runs smoothly. They might register guests and set up technical equipment. They oversee vendors and staff to ensure everything goes according to plan. If there are any problems, the event planner handles them behind the scenes so that there is little disruption for guests. After the event concludes, the planner pays vendors and may gather feedback from attendees.

Some event planners specialize in specific types of events. Meeting planners organize large meetings for companies or organizations. Some specialize in industries such as health care, while others focus on in-person or online events. Convention planners handle large conventions and trade shows. Often, they are employees of a hotel or convention center, overseeing outside vendors and planners. Exhibition organizers oversee the setup and promotion of a company's displays at a show or expo. Some event planners work with people to plan celebrations, such as weddings, reunions, anniversaries, fundraising events, and product launches.

A Typical Workday

Rachel Mazzola is a corporate events manager at Tripleseat, a company that provides a catering and event management web-based platform for restaurants, hotels, and other venues. For most event planners like Mazzola, every day brings a new challenge. "One of the job perks you get to experience as an event planner is that no two days are ever the same,"[4] she says.

Some days, Mazzola works at her company's offices. She often coordinates the planning of multiple events at the same time, so being organized is essential. Mazzola starts each day by creating a plan for what she wants to accomplish that day. "Look ahead at your upcoming events and put together a to-do list based on deadlines or items that need immediate attention and set up any meetings needed to get it done,"[5] she says. This morning routine of reviewing schedules, timelines, and to-do lists helps Mazzola prioritize tasks and make sure nothing is forgotten.

Mazzola keeps track of her projects by creating an event checklist for each one. She checks off each item as she completes it. She might call vendors to confirm food and beverage selections, discuss room setup plans with a hotel manager, and place orders for signage with vendors. She carefully records and tracks budgets, order amounts, and shipping details.

Mazzola also spends time each day collaborating with her team to share event updates and progress. She follows up with vendors, venues, and the event team to share information and address any questions that have arisen during the planning process. Mazzola and her team will also use this time to discuss the items still needed to be completed for each event.

All this planning and preparation leads up to the day of the event. Event planners typically arrive early at the event location to oversee setup, manage vendors, and attend to every detail to ensure everything runs smoothly and as planned. Planners stay onsite during the event to address any last-minute issues, answer questions, and ensure that guests have an incredible experience.

Education and Training

Most event planning positions require the applicant to have a bachelor's degree. Although a specific degree is not required, degrees in event management, hospitality management, public relations, marketing, business, communications, or a related field provide a solid foundation for an event planning career.

Formal education is just one part of preparing to be an event planner. Many employers prefer to hire candidates who have prior practical experience in event planning. Experience can be gained

A Vision Comes to Life

"It's an incredible feeling to spend months if not a full year planning, and coming up with ideas, just to see them come to life. Not only do they come to life, other people get to enjoy all that fun planning you've been doing. I love to see an event space be completely blank and by the end of the day it's a festival! It's glorious to see people from all walks of life come together to party for a common cause."

—Jennifer Grogan, owner of Peak Events

Jennifer Grogan, "Why Do I Love Event Planning?," Peak Events, February 15, 2023. https://peakeventsaz.com.

from working in the hospitality industry, including hotels, convention centers, and conferences. One can also gain valuable experience through internships, volunteering, or working in catering, event coordination, or venue management. Networking with experienced event planners or job shadowing can also provide valuable insight into event planning and help interested people find opportunities in the field.

Some people interested in working in event planning earn voluntary certifications. Common certifications include the Certified Meeting Professional, Certified Special Events Professional, and the Certified Professional in Catering and Events. Earning certifications demonstrates a person's specific skills or knowledge in meeting and event planning and can help that individual stand out from other candidates. "I have my Certified Meetings Professional (CMP) Certification, as well as my Digital Event Strategist (DES) certification. Both have been instrumental in helping plan multiple conferences a year, several of which are hybrid,"[6] says Belinda Hanson, operations and programs senior manager at the International Society for Computational Biology.

A couple meets with an event planner to discuss the venue and other plans for their wedding reception. Event planners work closely with their clients and vendors as they plan and organize all sorts of gatherings.

Many event planners build a portfolio to show potential clients or employers their work and experience. The portfolio includes details about the events worked, roles and responsibilities, and the event outcomes. Testimonials from satisfied clients are also beneficial in a portfolio.

Skills and Personality

Event planners need a wide range of skills to successfully organize and manage events. One of the most important is organization. Planners must keep track of multiple details simultaneously, including schedules, budgets, and vendor contacts. Time management is also key, since deadlines must be met and multiple events may be in progress at the same time.

Strong communication skills are also essential. Event planners must communicate effectively with clients, vendors, and team members to ensure that everyone understands the plan. They also need to be good listeners so they can understand the client's vision and needs. Being creative helps them design unique and exciting events that guests will remember.

Problem-solving is another important skill. Events do not always go as planned, so planners must be able to stay calm under pressure and find quick solutions. "Attendees don't see the moments of panic going on inside our heads. When things go wrong, it's important to stop, breathe, and find solutions quickly. Ninety percent of the time, problems are fixed by simply acknowledging the issue, thanking people for their patience, and staying calm,"[7] says Hanson.

Event planners should also be detail-oriented, ensuring that every aspect of the event is carefully planned. Leadership and teamwork skills enable them to manage staff effectively and work well with others. Finally, flexibility and adaptability are valuable traits. Plans can change quickly, and a good event planner must be ready to adjust as needed to keep everything on track and ensure the event's success.

Workplace Settings

Event planners work full time in an office and on-site at event locations, such as hotels and convention centers. They regularly travel to view potential event locations in person, meet with vendors and clients, and attend the events they organize.

The day-to-day job can be fast-paced and demanding. Event planners juggle multiple events and deadlines every day. Many work at least forty hours a week, with additional hours in the days leading up to a major event. Event planners sometimes work at night and on weekends, especially during an event.

Employers and Pay

Event planners can work for a variety of companies and industries. Some work for event planning companies, overseeing events for

Networking Pays Off

"In the beginning, it was difficult to get clients. I was new and didn't have much to show for events I've done. I *do* think it helped that when I first started, I was just planning smaller events and not weddings. . . . In order to connect with brides, I networked, networked, networked . . . and then networked some more! I went to every networking event I could, as well as introduced myself to others in the business that I wanted to work with. This is still my biggest piece of advice for those newer to the industry."

—Carisa Lockery, owner of Pink Olive Events

Quoted in Sarah Cavanagh, "Meet QC Event School Graduate, Carisa Lockery!," Pointers for Planners, June 30, 2023. www.qceventplanning.com.

multiple clients. Others work for civic, charitable, or professional organizations that regularly host events. Some event planners are self-employed and own their own event planning business. According to the Bureau of Labor Statistics' (BLS) *Occupational Outlook Handbook*, the median annual wage for event planners was $59,440 as of May 2024.

What Is the Future Outlook for Event Planners?

According to the BLS, job opportunities for meeting, convention, and event planners are projected to grow by 7 percent through 2033. This rate is faster than the projected 4 percent average growth rate for all occupations. Event planners will continue to be in demand by people who want help planning personal events such as weddings. In addition, businesses and organizations will need meeting and event planners to help host events.

Find Out More

American Association of Certified Wedding Planners (AACWP)

https://aacwp.org

The AACWP is a nonprofit organization dedicated to training wedding planners and providing opportunities to collaborate with other industry professionals. Its website has information about training and certification, continuing education, and networking events.

Event Marketer

www.eventmarketer.com

Event Marketer is an industry magazine that provides information and content for the event marketing and trade show industries. Its website provides news, trends, and case studies for event planning professionals.

Meeting Professionals International (MPI)

www.mpi.org

The MPI is one of the largest associations for event and meeting professionals. Its website offers information about certifications, event planning resources, networking events, educational resources, and industry news.

Special Events

www.specialevents.com

This website offers event planning industry news, event inspiration, trends, and resources. Every year, it stages the Special Event conference, a major annual gathering for planners.

Registered Nurse

What Does a Registered Nurse Do?

A registered nurse (RN) is a health care professional who plays an essential role in patient care. Most RNs work as part of a health care team that includes doctors, nurses, and other health care specialists. RNs work in hospitals, clinics, nursing homes, schools, and even in patients' homes. They are on the front lines of health care, working directly with patients and their families. Their primary responsibility is to care for people who are sick, injured, or recovering from surgery or illness. RNs also help people stay healthy by providing education and preventive care.

At a Glance

Number of Jobs
3.3 million in 2023

Pay
$93,600 median pay in 2024

Educational Requirements
Associate degree in nursing

Personal Qualities
Critical thinking, good communicator, organizational skills, compassionate, detail-oriented

Working Conditions
Hospitals, doctor offices, outpatient clinics, nursing care facilities

Future Job Outlook
Growth of 6 percent through 2033

One of the most essential duties of RNs is to monitor patients. They check a patient's vital signs such as heart rate, blood pressure, and temperature. RNs also observe patients for changes in their condition and report their observations to doctors and other health care professionals. RNs may help perform medical tests, administer medications, and insert and manage IVs. RNs also assist doctors during exams and procedures.

Registered nurses work closely with patients and their families. They explain diagnoses, help manage pain, and provide emotional support. They often teach patients how to care for themselves at home, such as how to take medications or manage chronic conditions like diabetes or asthma.

Alicia Rosiu decided to become an RN after her mother was diagnosed with cancer. She noticed the way that the nurses compassionately tended to her mother throughout her cancer treatment. As an RN, Rosiu has worked in a state prison, caring for patients of all backgrounds. "I love that nursing gives me the opportunity to reach patients across all walks of life," she says. "We get to be there and make a difference when patients are in pain, when they get good news and when they lose loved ones. This allows me to make brief connections, but still make a meaningful impact on the patients and family members I see."[8]

A Typical Workday

A typical workday for an RN is busy, fast-paced, and focused on patient care. Most RNs work in hospitals, clinics, or nursing homes, and their shifts often last eight to twelve hours. For RNs working in hospitals or other twenty-four-hour care facilities, the day usually begins with reviewing a handoff report from the previous shift, which outlines each patient's condition, medications, and any recent changes. Likewise, RNs working in outpatient clinics review the medical files for each patient they will see that day.

Throughout the day, RNs check patients' vital signs, such as blood pressure, heart rate, and temperature. They give medications and assist with treatments. In hospitals and other care facilities, RNs help patients with daily needs such as eating, bathing, and walking. RNs keep detailed records of patient appointments and daily progress. RNs also work closely with doctors and other health care team members, sharing updates on a patient's condition and implementing patient care plans. If a patient experiences a health emergency, RNs respond quickly and often take lifesaving action.

In addition to patient care, RNs provide emotional support to patients and their families. They comfort patients who are scared or in pain. They offer support and guidance to families during difficult times. At the end of their shift, RNs prepare reports on patients for the nurses on the next shift. They ensure that all patient records are updated to prevent gaps in patient care.

Marie Hasty worked as an RN in a medical intensive care unit (MICU), a specialized unit in a hospital that provides care for patients with serious illnesses or injuries. Hasty often worked on the night shift in the MICU. She says:

> Night shifts have a different rhythm compared to days, since the focus is on allowing patients to rest and continuing the plan of care. A typical night shift on my cardiac unit started with handoffs on our four to five patients, which usually took about 20 minutes. Then for the next two to four hours, I'd be passing medications, seeing patients, and charting my assessments. I might be in and out of a patient's room throughout the night if they needed frequent blood sugar checks, if they were unstable, or if they were on IV medication. In the morning, around 4 a.m., things would pick up again and I'd do another med pass before getting everything ready for the morning handoff.[9]

Education and Training

To become a registered nurse, a person needs to complete a nursing program and pass a licensing exam. Some RNs earn an associate of science in nursing (ASN), while others complete a bachelor of science in nursing (BSN). Some people earn a diploma from an approved nursing program offered by a hospital or medical center; completing the ASN typically takes two to three years. Nursing education includes classes in anatomy, physiolo-

Part of a Team

"I chose to become a nurse because I wanted to work as part of a team. Working together with peers to achieve difficult goals is incredibly gratifying. I love how we are always learning from each other. . . . Healthcare is an incredibly complex field, and no one person can know everything. We work together to share our knowledge to take better care of our patients."

—Luke Wigley, registered nurse

Quoted in Baylor Scott and White Health, "Why I Love Being a Nurse: 5 RNs Share What Nursing Means to Them," *Scrubbing In* (blog), Baylor Scott & White Health, May 9, 2022. www.bswhealth.com.

gy, psychology, microbiology, and social and behavioral sciences. It also includes hands-on clinical experiences.

Some hospitals prefer RNs with at least a bachelor's degree. RNs who graduated from an ASN or diploma program can earn a bachelor's degree through an RN-to-BSN program. Some RNs choose to earn a master of science in nursing or a doctor of nursing practice or doctor of philosophy in nursing, especially those who want to pursue leadership or research positions.

After completing educational requirements, RNs must pass the National Council Licensure Examination. Along with passing the exam, the candidates must also pass a criminal background check and meet various state licensing requirements. When all requirements are met, the state where they work will issue their license.

Some RNs earn certifications in specialties such as pediatrics or gerontology. Many RNs also earn certifications in cardiopulmonary resuscitation, basic life support, or advanced cardiac life support. They also complete continuing education throughout their career to stay current with medical knowledge and practices.

Registered nurses play an essential role in patient care. They have many duties, including checking vital signs, observing and reporting changes in a patient's condition, and managing or assisting with medical procedures and tests.

Skills and Personality

Successful RNs must be effective communicators, possess strong organizational skills, and remain calm in stressful situations. RNs must clearly explain medical information to patients and their families. They work closely with doctors and other health care professionals, communicating updates on a patient's condition. RNs must also be good listeners to understand patients' concerns. For Doug Fuentes, one of the most important parts of being an RN is making sure every patient and family member feels like they are being heard, especially when they are navigating a difficult medical diagnosis. "It's just listening to them and talking to them. It's doing a little thing like getting someone a warm blanket," he says. "Sometimes people just need to talk and they just need that ear . . . and you just let them talk. Sit with them for five to 10 minutes, and they are feeling better about things. They feel like they are being understood."[10]

Critical thinking is another essential skill for RNs, since nurses often need to make quick decisions in stressful situations. Organization and time-management skills are also crucial, because RNs frequently care for multiple patients simultaneously. Attention to detail can help nurses provide safe, effective care for each patient.

Every day, RNs work with patients who are sick, scared, or in pain. Caring for patients with compassion and empathy can make a big difference in a patient's experience in the hospital or clinic. Patience is also essential, because RNs often must deal with difficult or emotional situations. Medical emergencies can flare without warning, so RNs must be able to display calmness under pressure so they can care for patients effectively.

Workplace Settings

RNs work in various health care facilities, including hospitals, physicians' offices, and outpatient care centers. Some nurses work in home health care, traveling to patients' homes to provide care. Other nurses provide care in rehabilitation facilities, nursing homes, schools, community centers, and other sites. Some nurses travel to foreign countries to help patients in places where there is a shortage of health care workers.

RNs who work in hospitals and other health care facilities that provide twenty-four-hour care typically work in shifts. They may work days, nights, weekends, and holidays. Sometimes, they may be on call, which means they can be called into work with little notice. RNs who work in physicians' offices, schools, and other places that do not provide twenty-four-hour care typically work regular business hours. They may work some weekends if their workplace has weekend hours.

Addiction Recovery Nursing

"Addiction recovery nursing is one of a kind. First, you don't work in a hospital—you work in a facility that resembles a cozy home or a tranquil meditation retreat. Some luxury facilities even have pools, gyms, and personal chefs for the patients. Just like in other psychiatric nursing setups, it's not bedside care. Typically, two nurses handle over 20 patients—one for medications and one for charting. Job perks include the ability to establish meaningful connections with patients and make a difference. The challenge is that patients are often highly med-seeking, and educating them on healthy coping strategies is a struggle."

—Ann Real, registered nurse

Quoted in Marie Hasty, "A Day in the Life of a Nurse, According to Nurses," IntelyCare, 2025. www.intelycare.com.

Employers and Pay

RNs can work in a variety of health care facilities. Some of the largest employers include hospitals (58 percent); ambulatory health care services (19 percent); government programs (6 percent); nursing and residential care facilities (5 percent); and educational services (3 percent). According to the Bureau of Labor Statistics' (BLS) *Occupational Outlook Handbook*, the median annual wage for RNs was $93,600 as of May 2024.

What Is the Future Outlook for Registered Nurses?

According to the BLS, job opportunities for RNs are projected to grow by 6 percent through 2033. This rate is faster than the projected average growth rate of 4 percent for all occupations. As the number of older people increases, the demand for health care services is also projected to increase, as older adults typically need more medical attention than younger people. The need for RNs is projected to grow across many health care facilities, including hospitals and outpatient care centers. RNs will also be needed to treat older people in their homes or residential care facilities.

Find Out More

American Association of Critical-Care Nurses (AACN)

www.aacn.org

The AACN supports nurses working in critical-care settings. Its website provides resources, education, and networking opportunities for nurses.

American Nurses Association (ANA)

www.nursingworld.org/ana

The ANA supports nurses at all stages of their careers. Its website has information about continuing education, certification, standards, events, and more.

National League for Nursing (NLN)

www.nln.org

The NLN is an organization that supports nursing education and development. Its website provides industry news, teaching resources, certification, networking events, and more.

National Student Nurses' Association (NSNA)

www.nsna.org

The NSNA is a resource for nursing students who are seeking networking opportunities and information about potential career pathways. Its website has career planning guides, information about scholarships, and other student resource guides.

Hotel and Lodging Manager

What Does a Hotel and Lodging Manager Do?

Hotel and lodging managers are responsible for overseeing the daily operations of a hotel, motel, resort, or other lodging facility. Their main priority is to ensure that guests have a pleasant and safe stay while keeping the business functioning properly and profitably. Hotel and lodging managers wear many hats on the job. They welcome guests and ensure a smooth check-in process. Lodging managers provide superior service to their guests by handling any concerns or complaints and resolving problems quickly.

Hotel and lodging managers supervise all staff. In larger hotels, general managers may oversee assistant managers, including front desk managers, who focus on guest services at the hotel's front desk. Hotel managers hire, train, and manage hotel employees, including front desk clerks, housekeeping staff, maintenance workers, and food service employees. Managers schedule staff to ensure that the hotel's operations run smoothly twenty-four hours a day, seven days a week. They also evaluate staff performance.

Hotel and lodging managers also oversee the maintenance of their facilities. They make sure all guest rooms,

At a Glance

Number of Jobs
53,300 in 2023

Pay
$68,130 median pay in 2024

Educational Requirements
High school diploma or equivalent

Personal Qualities
Good communicator, organizational skills, customer service skills, problem-solving skills

Working Conditions
Hotels and motels

Future Job Outlook
Growth of 10 percent through 2033

conference rooms, fitness centers, pools, restaurants, and other areas are clean, safe, and in good condition. They verify that the equipment throughout the hotel is operating as required. They schedule and oversee any repairs or maintenance that are required.

Some hotel and lodging managers also manage a hotel's finances. They may set room rates and prepare budgets. They review and analyze income and expenses and come up with ideas to boost bookings, reduce costs, and increase profitability. They help promote the hotel through advertising, special offers, and online marketing. Some hotel managers monitor guest reviews and respond as needed.

Hotel and lodging managers are also responsible for ensuring that the hotel follows all required health, safety, and legal codes and standards. They ensure that the property complies with fire codes, labor laws, and other hospitality regulations. Overall, hotel and lodging managers juggle many tasks to provide great guest experiences while keeping the business efficient and commercially successful.

A Typical Day

Hotel managers begin their workdays early. They review overnight updates, including guest feedback and occupancy rates. They meet briefly with department leaders to plan the day, which may include handling guest needs, organizing staff shifts, or preparing for scheduled events. Throughout the day, hotel managers interact with guests, respond to questions or special requests, and make sure the hotel provides top-quality service. Managers also inspect guest rooms, dining areas, and other public spaces to make sure everything is clean and meets company standards. In between meetings, hotel managers review financial reports, looking for ways to cut expenses and increase revenues. They might have a meeting with marketing staff to plan hotel promotions and events.

When problems arise, such as maintenance issues or guest complaints, hotel managers act fast to fix them and protect the hotel's reputation. In the evening, managers check that everything is running efficiently. They might attend events to connect with guests or local businesses.

David Foschi is the general manager of the Hotel Bernini Palace, a five-star hotel in Florence, Italy. He describes a typical day, saying:

> My day starts early: I get to the hotel at eight o'clock and go straight to the Front Office, where the secretaries fill me in on the flow of guests and room occupancies. Then I go to the Booking Department, where I check the emails even before our booking operators start arriving. After that, I pop in at the breakfast department, the administration offices and the other departments, where I discuss things with the heads and the staff in general. I move about a lot and I try to be active. If needed, I try to lend everyone a hand, maintenance staff and porters included. The moment of the day I enjoy least is the paperwork I'm forced to do, but nothing fills me with satisfaction as much as direct contact with people.[11]

Education and Training

Hotel and lodging managers usually need to have at least a high school diploma. Students interested in becoming hotel managers should take classes in hospitality management if offered at their school. Some hotels prefer to hire people with a bachelor of science in hospitality management from a four-year college or university. In these programs, students will take classes in hotel management, accounting, marketing, and sales. Many programs will also include classes on hospitality computer software programs that are used in reservations, billing, and housekeeping management.

Resort Opening

"Currently, I am preparing for a resort opening, so I feel like I'm working on a massive puzzle board where every piece needs to fit perfectly. A good day at work for me is when I see everything coming together seamlessly, when the team is working together like a well-oiled machine. I love the challenge and the sense of accomplishment that comes with it. There's a certain thrill that comes with problem-solving and overcoming obstacles, and that's what keeps me motivated."

—Caitie L., general manager at the Lampung Marriott Resort & Spa

Quoted in Jason Yingling, "How a Marriott General Manager Built Her Global Career on a Foundation of Belonging," *The Life at Marriott Blog*, February 26, 2024. https://life.marriott.com.

Many people who want to become hotel managers get started in the hospitality industry by working jobs and gaining experience in guest services, as front desk staff, or in other hospitality positions. Some candidates learn the trade through internships or management trainee programs.

Obi J. worked his way through the ranks to become a hotel manager at the Ritz–Carlton in Orlando, Florida. Obi began his career in hospitality as an eighteen-year-old server in one of the Ritz–Carlton's restaurants. Obi's hard work and dedication helped him advance at the hotel from restaurant server to other positions, including restaurant manager, director of outdoor dining operations, banquet director, and director of food and beverage. In the summer of 2024, he was promoted to hotel manager. "In my experience, striving to be the best in every role I have has opened up new doors of opportunity for me. When I started as a server here, I used to stay late and organize our side stations or be the last one to go home after a long, busy day," he says. Obi has

> ### Cruise Ships: Hotels at Sea
>
> "With a moving hotel, there are a whole lot more challenges that come our way that static hotels or resorts just do not have to contend with. One day, we may have to skip a port where we were to load vital food stores. We would then have to move quickly to revise our menus and plan future ordering to make sure passengers are not impacted, and in fact have no idea this has happened. The next day, we may have an on board wedding to plan for or be preparing for the next turnaround."
>
> —Richard Harry, hotel general manager of the *Ruby Princess* cruise ship
>
> Quoted in World of Cruising, "Life On-Board with the Hotel General Manager of Ruby Princess," April 17, 2025. www.worldofcruising.co.uk.

participated in several training and development programs at the hotel, which helped prepare him for his management role. "One of the most helpful programs was the Emerging Leader Program (ELP) at The Ritz-Carlton, which gave me a better understanding of my role as a senior leader. Another great experience was attending the Marriott Boot Camp for senior executives, where I made valuable connections with people I still keep in touch with today,"[12] he says.

Some hotel managers earn professional certifications. These certifications are voluntary, but acquiring them can help individuals stand out to potential employers. Some certifications held by hotel managers include the Certified Hotel Administrator, Certified Hospitality Supervisor, and Certified Hospitality Manager.

Skills and Personality

A successful hotel manager must be a strong leader. Hotel managers guide and motivate staff, solve problems quickly, and make important decisions. They also need strong communication skills to speak clearly with guests, employees, and vendors. Organization is another key skill, since managers must handle schedules, budgets, events, and daily operations simultaneously. Attention to detail is also essential, because hotel managers strive to make every part of a guest's experience perfect, from the cleanliness of the room to participation in an event. General business skills are also helpful when budgeting and reviewing the hotel's profitability.

Customer service skills are essential, because a hotel manager's primary goal is to ensure that guests are happy. This means being polite, helpful, and ready to solve complaints calmly. Problem-solving skills help managers handle unexpected situations, such as maintenance issues or booking errors.

Hotel managers should be friendly, confident, and patient. A positive attitude helps keep staff motivated and creates a welcoming atmosphere for guests. They also need to be flexible and calm under pressure, especially during busy seasons or emergencies. "Many of my [general manager] friends will agree with me when I say, it's a unique job that requires a variety of skills with people, critical thinking, communication, organization, computer and financial competence all playing a part at making your hotel the best hotel for the guests, the team and the owners,"[13] says Mihir Bhatt, an experienced hotel manager.

Workplace Settings

Hotel and lodging managers work in hotels, motels, and other lodging facilities. Most work full time. Their hours may vary and can include nights, weekends, and holidays. Many hotel managers are on call twenty-four hours a day in case a problem arises at their facility. "I'm always available and in the event of problems, they can call me at all hours,"[14] says David Foschi. Travel for meetings and trade shows is common. In some resort hotels, the managers live on-site.

Employers and Pay

Most hotel managers work for hotels and motels. Others work for casinos, RV parks, recreational camps, hostels, or bed and breakfasts. According to the Bureau of Labor Statistics' (BLS) *Occupational Outlook Handbook*, the median annual salary for hotel and lodging managers was $68,130 as of May 2024. However, pay often depends on the type and size of the facility and its location.

What Is the Future Outlook for Hotel and Lodging Managers?

According to the BLS, job opportunities for hotel and lodging managers are projected to grow by 10 percent through 2033. This rate is faster than the projected 4 percent average growth rate for all occupations. Strong projections for travel spending will lead to demand for lodging managers in hotels and other facilities. Projected growth in demand for extended-stay accommodations, as well as business and leisure travel, is expected to drive increased demand for hotel and lodging managers.

Find Out More

American Hotel & Lodging Association (AHLA)

www.ahla.com

The AHLA is a national trade organization that represents the US hotel and lodging industry. It supports businesses of all sizes, from major hotel chains to small, independent properties. Its website offers industry news, events, reports, and a resource library.

Hospitality Sales and Marketing Association International (HSMAI)

https://global.hsmai.org

The HSMAI is a global organization dedicated to supporting professionals in hospitality sales, marketing, and revenue management. Its website has information about industry news, education, certification, and more.

International Hotel & Restaurant Association (IHRA)

https://ih-ra.com

The IHRA is a global organization that represents the interests of the hospitality and tourism industry worldwide, including hotels, restaurants, and related businesses. Its website has the latest industry news and events. There is also a section devoted to best practices to keep businesses environmentally sustainable.

Personal Financial Advisor

What Does a Personal Financial Advisor Do?

Personal financial advisors help clients meet their financial goals. They evaluate their clients' financial situation and guide them through various investment, tax, and insurance decisions. Advisors get to know their clients and help them create budgets and plan for short- and long-term financial goals. They help clients create a road map to achieve their goals, such as buying a house, paying for college, and saving for retirement.

At a Glance

Number of Jobs
321,000 in 2023

Pay
$102,140 median pay in 2024

Educational Requirements
Bachelor's degree

Personal Qualities
Analytical mind, math skills, interpersonal skills, communication skills, organizational skills

Working Conditions
Office

Future Job Outlook
Growth of 17 percent through 2033

Many personal financial advisors help clients decide how to invest their money. They talk with clients about different types of investments, such as stocks, bonds, mutual funds, and annuities. They discuss the risks and taxes associated with each type of investment and develop an investment plan that meets the client's goals. Many personal financial advisors also sell insurance products, such as life or long-term disability insurance, to their clients.

Personal financial advisors monitor their clients' investments regularly. They research new investment opportunities to determine whether they are a good fit for their clients. Personal financial advisors meet with clients at least annually to talk about any life changes or updates to a client's goals. They review their clients' financial portfolios and make any necessary adjustments to investments or insurance to keep the clients on track to meet planned goals. Many personal financial advisors have a license that allows them to directly buy and sell financial products, including stocks, bonds, and annuities. Some clients have an agreement with their advisor that allows the advisor to make decisions about buying and selling stocks and bonds in their financial portfolio when opportunities arise or financial markets change.

A significant aspect of a personal financial advisor's role is educating clients about complex financial topics. They discuss the stock and bond markets and how these investments can generate financial returns. They explain investment risk, clarify why some options are riskier than others, and help clients determine the level of risk they are comfortable taking with their portfolio. Financial advisors also show clients how their financial decisions affect the taxes they owe. With all this information, clients can make better-informed financial decisions.

Some personal financial advisors also help clients with estate planning. Estate planning ensures that a client's assets are managed and transferred as they wish after their death or disability. Estate planning can also make sure a client's estate is structured to minimize the taxes beneficiaries will have to pay.

A Typical Workday

A typical day for a personal financial advisor often involves balancing responsibilities and clients. Part of the day is spent reaching out to prospective clients by cold-calling, conducting in-person meetings, attending community events, or marketing online. Advisors will also reach out to referrals from existing clients.

Personal financial advisors also spend time each day on client management. This includes meeting with clients in person or online, answering client questions via phone or email, reviewing client portfolios, or sending out email communications to a client list. Spending time on client management keeps existing clients happy and more likely to refer an advisor to friends and family.

Advisors spend a large part of their day working on financial plans for clients. Financial planning is the heart of the job. Clients depend on financial advisors to create personalized plans to meet their financial goals. To create personalized financial plans, advisors might create models that evaluate different investment scenarios. When clients have a life change, advisors update these models with new information. They also review timelines to evaluate how well the plan is working to meet the client's financial goals. The more the advisor understands each client's life situation and goals, the more effective they can be at financial planning.

Personal financial advisors also keep up with changes in the financial service industry. They learn new skills and review regulatory and industry trends. Sometimes, advisors attend conferences or workshops to keep their skills current.

Arianna P. works as a personal financial advisor at Vanguard, an investment management company. "A typical day in my role as an advisor includes having phone conversations with clients and helping them meet their long-term financial goals through Vanguard's methodology and investment strategy. I assist clients with a variety of topics including retirement planning, investment planning, and more," she says. "My favorite part of each day is hearing from clients that I was able to help them achieve peace of mind following our conversation."[15]

Education and Training

People who want to become a personal financial advisor should earn a bachelor's degree in finance, accounting, or a related business major. Students should take classes in accounting, investments, taxes, estate planning, and risk management. These subjects will help students understand basic accounting, financial markets, and

Helping Clients Achieve Goals

"One of the most fulfilling aspects of my job is meeting new people. Our firm is centered around enriching the lives of others—including our clients, colleagues, and the community through active service opportunities. I also love the opportunity to meet someone who is questioning how to best prepare for retirement. This gives me a chance to learn more about their unique situation, their goals, and craft a plan specifically designed to help them achieve their retirement dream. As the relationship progresses, my greatest fulfillment is when the client can see that dream coming to fruition and they can accomplish their goals."

—Michael Wagner, personal financial advisor at the Welch Group

Quoted in Brent Gillis, "Why I Became a Financial Advisor," Welch Group, December 14, 2022. https://welchgroup.com.

investment strategies. A master of business administration degree or master of finance degree can be beneficial, helping a person strengthen financial skills and stand out to potential employers.

When they first start working, personal financial advisors get on-the-job training. Typically, they work closely with senior advisors and learn the details of the job, including how to build a client list, develop investment portfolios, and perform other tasks. Most new advisors will work under the supervision of a senior advisor for at least a year.

In addition to educational requirements, most personal financial advisors must be licensed. Advisors who directly buy or sell stocks or bonds must pass licensing exams. Advisors who give investment advice may need to register with the US Securities and Exchange Commission or a state regulatory agency. Those who sell insurance products must be licensed by a state board.

Many personal financial advisors earn certifications to enhance their skills and competencies. To earn a Certified Financial Planner certification, the advisor must earn a bachelor's degree, have several

Personal financial advisors help clients meet their financial goals. They evaluate their clients' financial situation and guide them through various investment, tax, and insurance decisions.

years of relevant experience, and pass an exam. Other helpful certifications include the Chartered Financial Consultant or Chartered Financial Analyst. To maintain their licenses and certifications, personal financial advisors regularly complete continuing education classes. These classes enable them to stay up-to-date with the latest industry practices, regulations, and trends.

Skills and Personality

Several skills are essential for success as a personal financial advisor. Their primary role is to develop a customized investment portfolio for clients. To do this successfully, they need to have strong analytical skills to review and analyze financial information, economic trends, regulatory information, and more. Because they work with numbers as they create and manage investment plans, advisors should also have strong math skills. Financial advisors often juggle multiple clients and tasks every day. Therefore, they must be organized and able to prioritize and manage their time effectively.

A significant part of the job involves working directly with people, both current and prospective clients. They interact with clients daily, explaining complex financial concepts to those without a finance background. To do this, advisors should have strong interpersonal and communication skills so they can talk to people of all backgrounds and make them feel comfortable and heard. Their ability to listen to clients, understand their individual needs, and provide personalized financial advice is essential. Valerie Leonard, chief executive officer of EverThrive Financial Group, says:

> Successful financial advisors . . . take a genuine interest in their clients' lives. I also often hear from prospective clients that they haven't heard from their advisor in quite some time. In my opinion, if the client truly comes first, their advisor would be in regular communication, educating them each time they talk, making sure they are comfortable with the strategies in place, and checking in to be sure the client's needs or goals have not changed.[16]

Workplace Settings

Personal financial advisors typically work in an office environment. They may travel to attend workshops and conferences. They may also attend networking events to meet prospective clients. Most advisors work full time and, depending on their client load, may work more than forty hours per week. While most work during regular business hours, they sometimes have client meetings in the evenings or on weekends to accommodate clients' schedules.

Employers and Pay

Personal financial advisors work for a variety of employers. Some are self-employed and have their own advising business. Some of the largest employers include securities, commodities, and other

Blending the Analytical and the Personal

"Personal finance was right for me [as a college major]. It had the technical, analytical, and economic side of things, but it also had the human, emotional, and personal elements. It blended them perfectly.

I could nerd out in spreadsheets with numbers while hearing someone's life story, what was important to them, and what they were concerned about.

Personal finance felt like a giant puzzle with hundreds of ways each person's puzzle could be put together. None of them were right or wrong. They simply prioritized different elements.

As I continued taking courses, it only became clearer I made the right choice."

—Elliott Appel, personal financial advisor at Kindness Financial Planning

Elliott Appel, "Why I Became a Financial Planner," Kindness Financial Planning, July 11, 2022. https://kindnessfp.com.

financial investment firms (60 percent); credit intermediation firms (16 percent); insurance carriers (3 percent); and professional, scientific, and technical services firms (3 percent). The Bureau of Labor Statistics' (BLS) *Occupational Outlook Handbook* indicates that the median annual salary for personal financial advisors was $102,140 as of May 2024.

What Is the Future Outlook for Personal Financial Advisors?

According to the BLS, job opportunities for personal financial advisors are projected to grow by 17 percent in the United States through 2033. This rate is faster than the projected average growth rate of 4 percent for all occupations. The main driver of growth is the aging of the US population. As the baby boomer generation retires, they will need financial planning advice, increasing the demand for personal financial advisors. Additionally, as more people live longer, the need for financial planning services will also increase.

The increasing shift of companies away from defined benefit pension plans for their employees means that people will need to save and invest more for retirement themselves. This will also increase the demand for personal financial advisors. Although computer programs that provide automated investment advice may partially cut into that demand, industry experts project that most people still prefer a human advisor for complex and personalized investment advice.

Find Out More

Certified Financial Planner Board of Standards

www.cfp.net

The Certified Financial Planner Board of Standards is a nonprofit organization that sets and enforces professional standards for personal financial planners in the United States and awards the Certified Financial Planner certification. Its website has information about obtaining certification, applying for scholarships, and other candidate resources.

Financial Planning Association (FPA)

www.financialplanningassociation.org

The FPA is a leading professional organization for certified financial planners and others involved in financial planning. Its website has information for financial planners in all stages of their careers, including education resources, networking opportunities, research, news, and more.

National Association of Personal Financial Advisors (NAPFA)

www.napfa.org

The NAPFA is a professional organization for financial advisors. The NAPFA website has education resources, scholarship opportunities, and a link to a monthly podcast.

Police Officer

What Does a Police Officer Do?

Police officers work in communities nationwide to maintain public safety, enforce laws, and protect lives and property. They perform a range of duties, such as responding to emergency and nonemergency calls, patrolling assigned areas, conducting traffic stops, and issuing citations or warnings for violations of the law. Police officers also investigate crimes. They collect, secure, and document evidence from crime scenes and question witnesses and people of interest. The police obtain and serve warrants to search homes, cars, and other places of interest during an investigation. As part of an investigation, the police conduct surveillance on people and places. They use criminal databases to search for information about vehicles, warrants, and arrest records. Police also arrest people suspected of committing crimes. They write detailed reports about their investigations. Police also work with district attorneys to provide information needed in a trial and will testify in court if needed.

At a Glance

Number of Jobs
796,800 in 2023

Pay
$77,270 median pay in 2024

Educational Requirements
High school diploma or equivalent

Personal Qualities
Physical strength and stamina, empathy, good communicator, analytical, leadership skills

Working Conditions
Station house offices, neighborhood streets, crime and accident scenes

Future Job Outlook
Growth of 4 percent through 2033

Police officers also participate in community outreach events to build a positive relationship with the community they protect. They work closely with other public agencies, including fire departments, emergency medical services, other law enforcement agencies, and community organizations. These efforts can build trust and cooperation between the police and community members, which can help keep everyone safer. "The most fulfilling part of the job for me is having the human interaction, interacting with community members,"[17] says Trooper David Holmquist with the Minnesota State Patrol.

Some police officers specialize in certain types of crimes or duties. Detectives focus on gathering facts and collecting evidence for serious crimes, such as robberies, assaults, and homicides. Some officers work in teams that focus on combating narcotics distribution or organized crime. Some police departments have specialized units, such as mounted or horseback officers, motorcycle officers, or special weapons and tactics (SWAT) units. Fish and game wardens patrol hunting and fishing areas to enforce wildlife and conservation laws. Some police officers may join the Federal Bureau of Investigation (FBI) and investigate federal and interstate crimes. Sometimes, these FBI agents will assist local police with investigations that cross state lines or involve federal jurisdiction.

A Typical Workday

Policing is a twenty-four-hour, seven-day-a-week job. Police officers work in shifts to ensure that there is always someone on duty to respond to calls for assistance. Most police departments divide the day into three shifts, also called watches, to cover the twenty-four hours. For example, the first shift might be 4:00 a.m. to 1:00 p.m., the second shift 12:00 p.m. to 8:00 p.m., and the third shift 8:00 p.m. to 5:00 a.m. Many police departments schedule officers to work four consecutive ten- to twelve-hour days, followed by three days off. Then, they repeat the rotation.

Communication Is Key

"When conducting traffic stops, street stops, and interrogating suspects, your most powerful weapon is effective communication. Your ability to talk and connect with citizens is paramount. If you are shy, don't like talking to strangers, and do not listen effectively, police work may NOT be for you.

In police work, you learn to adjust your style of communication based on the audience you are serving. From victims of crime to witnesses, to potential suspects, and to serious criminals (gang members, drug dealers), you MUST adjust your style for the right environment."

—Jeff Halstead, retired chief of police, Fort Worth, Texas

Quoted in Pedro Candela, "'Police Career Survival': Top 5 Tips for New Law Enforcement Officers," Genasys, August 21, 2024. https://genasys.com.

At the start of a shift, a patrol officers typically gather for roll call. This meeting can last about thirty minutes, and officers use the time to check in, learn about any assignments or tasks for the day, and get updates from supervisors about current cases and new alerts. After roll call, the officers will spend a few minutes inspecting their patrol car, making sure the tires and electronics operate as expected and the car is stocked with flares, first aid kits, and other safety equipment. Most patrol officers work in pairs in the community. As they are ready to patrol, they will contact the police dispatcher to signal that they are on duty.

The rest of the officers' day depends on what they encounter on their shift. As they patrol their assigned area, they might interact with community members. They might be called to respond to a 911 call or provide backup to other officers and first responders. If they see situations that could get out of control—such as a loud, angry argument between two people on the street—police officers intervene to reduce tensions. They might be called to a crime scene, where they take witness statements, investigate and gather evidence, and arrest suspects when necessary. At the end of their shift, all police officers write and file a report on the day's activities. "Every day is a little bit different, which is what I've always loved about law enforcement—the variety. It could be a crash. It could be working traffic enforcement, maybe making a presentation at a school or a community event, so it could really be a variety of things throughout the day,"[18] says Holmquist.

For Officer Jose Torres with the New York Police Department, one of the most memorable days on the job occurred when he was training new officers in the field. He explains:

> A call came in from a distraught mother whose one-year-old daughter had stopped breathing. At the time, I was working with a brand-new officer straight out of the academy. The two of us raced over and found the child lifeless in her mother's arms. We had to move quickly and be focused if we were going to save her life. I laid the little girl on the floor and started performing CPR [cardiopulmonary resuscitation]. My training just kicked in as the adrenaline was pumping through my body. All I could think about was getting her breathing again. When she took that first breath and opened her eyes, I felt an immense sense of relief. Seeing that child safely back in her mother's arms was the best feeling in the world.[19]

Education and Training

The process of becoming a police officer starts with a high school diploma or equivalent. Some police departments and federal law enforcement agencies require candidates to have a bachelor's degree. Some students choose to earn a bachelor's degree in criminal justice, security and protective services, social science, or a related major. For some police departments, knowing a foreign language that is widely spoken in the community is beneficial. Other requirements vary by community, but most departments require candidates to be at least twenty-one years old and in top physical condition. Those who go on to work for federal law enforcement agencies or some state and local agencies may have to prove US citizenship. Candidates for law enforcement jobs may be disqualified for having a felony conviction or a history of drug use.

Prospective police officers must successfully graduate from a police training academy. At the academy, candidates receive classroom instruction about civil rights, police ethics, and federal, state, and local laws. Candidates also receive hands-on training in firearm use, self-defense, first aid, and emergency response.

Most police officers start their careers as patrol officers. After a period of on-the-job training, officers are eligible to be promoted. Promotions to corporal, sergeant, lieutenant, and captain are based on job performance and passing a written test. Some officers can earn a promotion to detective or an assignment in a specialized unit.

Skills and Personality

To be a police officer, a person needs a strong set of physical, mental, and social skills. Physical fitness is essential for staying active on the job and handling emergencies. Problem-solving and critical thinking are essential for making quick, smart decisions, especially in high-pressure situations.

Officers also need strong communication skills to speak clearly, listen carefully, and interact respectfully with people from all backgrounds. "About 75 percent of the job is communication, especially as a patrol officer. If you can communicate with someone, then the rest comes easily. It really helps when you understand the communities, cultures, and backgrounds of the people you're trying to serve. On this job, you have to want to help people,"[20] says Torres.

A police officer sits with a child who became separated from her family at a parade. Police officers perform a range of duties including responding to emergency and nonemergency calls, patrolling assigned areas, conducting traffic stops, and issuing citations.

A good police officer must also be observant and detail-oriented to notice things that others might miss. Emotional control and patience help officers stay calm and professional, even during stressful encounters. Honesty, integrity, and a strong sense of responsibility are also key to earning the trust of the community. Teamwork is important too, since officers often work closely with others to keep communities safe.

Workplace Settings

Police officers work in a variety of settings, depending on their assignments. Many spend time patrolling communities in police vehicles or on foot. Some walk city streets; others cruise country roads or highways in patrol cars or on motorcycles. Police officers also spend

A Desire to Do Right

"In the middle of a situation, you have to be able to make a split-second decision, and you have to be able to make the right decision. You need good judgement and the desire to do the right things for the right reasons. You need to be a good communicator; 90% of the job is talking to people of all different cultures, walks of life, nationalities, genders, lifestyles, and you need to be accepting of everyone you come in contact with."

—Officer Ryan Cody-Berry, Seattle Police Department

Quoted in Omie Drawhorn, "Port Police Officer Wants to Make a Difference," Port of Seattle, August 31, 2022. www.portseattle.org.

time at police stations, completing paperwork, attending briefings, or handling investigations. Some may work in specialized units like K-9, SWAT, or detective divisions. Their job can involve indoor office work, but it frequently requires being outdoors in all types of weather and responding to emergencies. The workplace is fast-paced, is demanding, and can be dangerous or stressful at times.

Employers and Pay

Most police officers work for local, state, or federal government law enforcement agencies (96 percent). A few police officers work for state, local, and private educational services (4 percent). According to the Bureau of Labor Statistics' (BLS) *Occupational Outlook Handbook*, the median annual salary for police officers and detectives was $77,270 as of May 2024. That pay varies widely by location.

What Is the Future Outlook for Police Officers?

According to the BLS, job opportunities for police officers and detectives are projected to grow by 4 percent through 2033. This rate is about the same as the projected average growth rate for all occupations. An increased demand for public safety is expected to drive the need for more police officers. However, this demand will depend on state and local law enforcement budgets.

Find Out More

Discover Policing

www.discoverpolicing.org

Discover Policing is an informational website for those interested in a career in law enforcement. Its purpose is to let potential candidates know about police training, the hiring process, and exam preparation. A job database is also available.

Fraternal Order of Police (FOP)

https://fop.net

The FOP is the largest organization of sworn law enforcement officers in the United States. Its website has information about becoming a police officer and officer training.

Police1

www.police1.com

Police1 is a resource for police officers or those interested in pursuing a law enforcement career. While offering information on career readiness, the site also compiles news coverage, analysis of policing topics, and product guides.

What Does a Social Worker Do?

Social workers help people cope with challenges in their daily lives and connect them to the resources and support they need. A social worker's calling is to improve the well-being of individuals, families, and communities. Social workers often work with people who are experiencing difficult situations, such as poverty, abuse, addiction, illness, unemployment, or family dysfunction. They listen to clients' concerns, assess their needs, and develop plans to help them find solutions.

One of the key roles of social workers is to provide emotional support. They help people manage stress, process trauma, and work through mental health issues. In clinical settings, licensed social workers may offer counseling or therapy. In schools, they help students deal with bullying, academic pressure, or issues at home. In hospitals, they support patients dealing with serious illness or injury, helping them understand treatment options or arranging care after discharge. For Abigale Johnson, a licensed clinical social worker, the many roles of a social worker were surprising at first. "I didn't realize

At a Glance

Number of Jobs
751,900 in 2023

Pay
$61,330 median pay in 2024

Educational Requirements
Bachelor's degree

Personal Qualities
Compassionate, good communicator, organizational skills, and problem-solving skills

Working Conditions
Offices, schools, hospitals

Future Job Outlook
Growth of 7 percent through 2033

that there are so many places and populations that social workers service,"[21] she says.

Social workers also act as advocates. They help clients understand their rights; apply for services like housing assistance, food programs, or health care; and speak up for those who cannot speak for themselves. They often collaborate with other professionals like doctors, teachers, and law enforcement to ensure clients receive the best care and support.

Clinical social workers and licensed clinical social workers are certified to diagnose and treat mental, behavioral, and emotional disorders. They develop treatment plans with clients and provide therapy, working with them to help change problem behaviors and cope with difficult situations.

A Typical Workday

A typical workday for social workers depends on where they work and the clients they serve. Many social workers start the day by reviewing their current cases and checking to see whether there were any texts, calls, voicemails, or email messages received from clients overnight. Throughout the day, they meet with clients and make home visits. They may also have meetings with other social workers to collaborate on cases and talk about ways to address a client's problems. They may meet with police officers or lawyers to talk about a client's case. For many social workers, communication and responding to messages from the clients they serve often takes up a significant part of the day.

Dalton Shump is a social worker and case manager for KVC Health Systems in Olathe, Kansas. He coordinates and supports the day-to-day needs of children and teens in foster care and their families. At any point, he works with up to twenty children or families. Shump says:

> A typical day for me [involves] having a few worker–child meetings. These are where we case managers visit our

> youth clients in their respective foster homes or relative homes monthly to see how they are doing and get any new updates. After those, I usually have at least one visit between a parent and child that I supervise in the afternoons or evenings. Depending on the time of the month, I might have a court hearing to attend in between those visits or a case plan meeting to hold. The rest of the time is trying to communicate with clients and schedule next month's meetings or handle daily crises.[22]

Education and Training

To become a social worker, candidates typically need at least a bachelor of social work (BSW) degree. This credential provides foundational knowledge in social work practices, human behavior, and social welfare policy. Some social workers may have degrees in related fields like psychology or sociology. However, for more advanced roles or to become a licensed clinical social worker, a master of social work (MSW) degree is usually required. An MSW allows a person to specialize in areas like mental health, school social work, or medical social work.

In addition to classroom learning, both BSW and MSW programs include supervised fieldwork or internships that provide students with hands-on experience working with clients and professionals in real-world settings. After completing their education, social workers must meet state licensing requirements, which usually include passing an exam and completing a set number of supervised work hours.

Continuing education is also important. Social workers often take courses throughout their careers to stay current on best practices and to maintain their licenses. Some social workers earn certifications by completing an educational component and

Building Connections

"I think the best thing about being a social worker is meeting people and hearing their stories. Connecting with others and building rapport is the part of the job which we all love and wish there was more of. It is such a privilege to gain insight into the life of another person. It brings me immense joy every time I go out on a visit. Some might think that's cheesy, but those who know me will know how excited I get every time I go out and get to put my social work skills into action!"

—Tilly Baden, adult social care manager

Quoted in *Social Work News*, "What's the Best and Worst Thing About Being a Social Worker?," January 22, 2024. www.mysocialworknews.com.

passing a written or practical exam. This combination of education, field training, and licensing prepares social workers to help people effectively in a wide variety of situations.

Skills and Personality

To be a successful social worker, a person needs a variety of important skills. Communication is one of the most essential. Social workers must be able to listen carefully to clients, speak clearly, and write reports and case notes accurately. Empathy is also crucial. Social workers need to understand and care about what others are going through even if they have not experienced it themselves. Critical thinking and problem-solving skills help social workers analyze complex situations and make good decisions for their clients.

Organization and time management are essential skills for social workers, who often handle multiple cases simultaneously and must maintain up-to-date records. Patience and a calm demeanor are also important. Social workers may work with people who are upset, angry, or in crisis, and they must stay calm and

A social worker meets with a young man to discuss his living situation. Social workers help people cope with challenges in their daily lives and connect them to the resources and support they need.

professional under pressure. They must also recognize the fact that they cannot solve every problem for every client. "Your job as a social worker is not to fix things for people. Your job is to help individuals process and find different ways of dealing with life issues,"[23] says social worker Christine Smith. Cultural sensitivity is necessary because social workers will often work with people from diverse backgrounds.

Finally, collaboration and teamwork are essential in social work. Social workers often work with other professionals—such as teachers, doctors, and law enforcement—to support their clients. These skills help social workers protect vulnerable individuals, provide support, and create positive changes in their communities.

Workplace Settings

Social workers can work in many different settings, depending on their specialty. Some work in schools, helping students with emotional, social, or academic problems. Others work in hospitals or health care centers, supporting patients and families through illness or injury. Child welfare agencies and government offices employ social workers to help protect children and support families. Some work in mental health clinics or rehabilitation centers, assisting people with addiction, trauma, or mental health challenges.

Social workers may also work in nursing homes, prisons, homeless shelters, or nonprofit organizations. Some even visit clients in their homes or the community. Their workplaces can be fast-paced and emotionally demanding, requiring flexibility and strong coping skills. "Social workers can have a higher rate of burnout depending on the population they work with and their job. For example, workers in child welfare and the foster care system have a higher turnover and burnout rate," says Catherine Pearlman, assistant professor of social work at the University of Massachusetts Global. "It's a highly rewarding job, but social workers must be mindful of their needs to make sure they don't get depleted,"[24] she adds.

Employers and Pay

Social workers work for a variety of employers depending on their focus and specialty. The largest employers of social workers in 2023 were individual and family service agencies (18 percent); local government agencies (14 percent); state government agencies (12 percent); educational services (10 percent); and community, emergency, and vocational rehabilitation services (3 percent). According to the Bureau of Labor Statistics' (BLS) *Occupational Outlook Handbook*, the median annual salary for social workers was $61,330 as of May 2024.

What Is the Future Outlook for Social Workers?

According to the BLS, job opportunities for social workers are projected to grow by 7 percent through 2033. This rate is faster than the projected 4 percent average growth rate for all occupations. In

Checking In at the Hospital

"I tell them my role is to check on the family and the patient, make sure they're doing OK, to see if there are any questions or concerns I can help address, and then to get a bit of information from them to make sure they have everything they need when they go home so that they and their child are safe and healthy. As soon as I say that and they hear my tone, they relax and we have a good conversation."

—Tara Atwood, a Children's Hospital Los Angeles social worker

Quoted in Jeff Weinstock, "What's a Social Worker? Here's the Truth About This Misunderstood Profession," Children's Hospital Los Angeles, March 12, 2024. www.chla.org.

particular, the demand for health care social workers is expected to increase as the US population ages in the next decade and their families need support and advice for new treatments, medications, and health concerns. As more people seek treatment for mental illness and substance abuse, the demand for social workers who specialize in these areas is also expected to increase. As the courts send more drug offenders to substance abuse treatment programs instead of prison, social workers who work in these programs will be needed.

Find Out More

Clinical Social Work Association

www.clinicalsocialworkassociation.org

The Clinical Social Work Association represents clinical social workers, especially those in private practice or mental health care. It provides advocacy, resources, and support for licensing and practice. Its website has information about current legislation, educational resources, and links to find a local clinical social worker.

Council on Social Work Education (CSWE)

www.cswe.org

The CSWE is the national accrediting body for social work education in the United States. It sets educational standards and promotes high-quality social work teaching and learning. On the website, students can explore social work and learn how to get started in a social work career.

National Association of Social Workers (NASW)

www.socialworkers.org

The NASW is the largest membership organization of professional social workers in the United States. Its website has news and information about various areas of social work practice.

Source Notes

Introduction: Why People Skills Matter

1. Quoted in Axes Physical Therapy, "Why Did I Choose Physical Therapy as a Profession?," September 16, 2024. https://axespt.com.
2. Quoted in Axes Physical Therapy, "Why Did I Choose Physical Therapy as a Profession?"
3. Quoted in Axes Physical Therapy, "Why Did I Choose Physical Therapy as a Profession?"

Event Planner

4. Rachel Mazzola, "A Day in the Life of a Corporate Event Planner," *EventUp* (blog), Tripleseat, February 11, 2021. https://eventupblog.tripleseat.com.
5. Mazzola, "A Day in the Life of a Corporate Event Planner."
6. Quoted in Meaghan Maybee, "A Day in the Life of an Event Planner: 5 Lessons Learned," *Tag Talk* (blog), pc/nametag, August 3, 2022. https://blog.pcnametag.com.
7. Quoted in Maybee, "A Day in the Life of an Event Planner."

Registered Nurse

8. Quoted in Baylor Scott and White Health, "Why I Love Being a Nurse: 5 RNs Share What Nursing Means to Them," *Scrubbing In* (blog), Baylor Scott & White Health, May 9, 2022. www.bswhealth.com.
9. Marie Hasty, "A Day in the Life of a Nurse, According to Nurses," IntelyCare, 2025. www.intelycare.com.
10. Quoted in Scott and White Health, "Why I Love Being a Nurse."

Hotel and Lodging Manager

11. Quoted in Hotel Bernini Palace, "The Manager Speaks." https://hotelbernini.duetorrihotels.com.
12. Quoted in Jason Yingling, "This Ritz–Carlton Hotel Manager Wants His Career Story to Inspire Other to Never Give

Up," *The Life at Marriott Blog*, August 20, 2024. https://life.marriott.com.
13. Mihir Bhatt, "Hi, My Name Is Mihir Bhatt, and I Have Been in Hotel Leadership for over Ten Years Now," LinkedIn, November 5, 2022. www.linkedin.com.
14. Quoted in Hotel Bernini Palace, "The Manager Speaks."

Personal Financial Advisor

15. Arianna P., "Starting My Career in Financial Advice at Vanguard," *Careers Blog*, Vanguard, June 18, 2025. www.vanguardjobs.com.
16. Quoted in Craig Anthony, "5 Traits of Successful Financial Advisors," Investopedia, May 9, 2024. www.investopedia.com.

Police Officer

17. Quoted in Minnesota Department of Public Safety, "Why They Chose the State Patrol, and Why You Should Too," August 1, 2025. https://dps.mn.gov.
18. Quoted in Minnesota Department of Public Safety, "Why They Chose the State Patrol, and Why You Should Too."
19. Quoted in John Jay College of Criminal Justice, "Behind the Badge: Army Vet and NYPD Officer Jose Torres '23 Leads with Mentorship," September 22, 2022. www.jjay.cuny.edu.
20. Quoted in John Jay College of Criminal Justice, "Behind the Badge."

Social Worker

21. Quoted in UMass Global, "7 Things to Know Before Becoming a Social Worker," July 29, 2025. www.umassglobal.edu.
22. Quoted in KVC Health Systems, "A Day in the Life of a Social Worker," March 24, 2021. www.kvc.org.
23. Quoted in UMass Global, "7 Things to Know Before Becoming a Social Worker."
24. Quoted in UMass Global, "7 Things to Know Before Becoming a Social Worker."

Interview with a Personal Financial Advisor

Megan Spear is a personal financial advisor at Spear, Tremaine and Associates, a private wealth advisory practice of Ameriprise Financial Services in Pittsburgh, Pennsylvania. She has worked as a personal financial advisor for twenty-seven years. She answered questions about her career by email.

Q: Why did you become a private wealth advisor?

A: I've always had an interest in math and accounting. After my college graduation, I began interviewing primarily with accounting firms. A family friend offered an interview at American Express Financial Advisors (now Ameriprise Financial) and shared the possibility of a career path in personal financial planning. The idea of working with people to help them reach their goals seemed very intriguing and rewarding.

Q: What education or experiences should someone in your career have?

A: I feel having a business degree is very important. With a business degree, you will likely have courses in accounting, finance, marketing, economics—all of which provide a solid foundation in financial planning. From there, it is so important to continue your education and obtain certifications to build on your knowledge and set you apart from other advisors. My certifications, for example, include:

CFP® CERTIFIED FINANCIAL PLANNER™
CRPC™ Chartered Retirement Planning Counselor™
APMA™ Accredited Portfolio Management Advisor™

Q: Can you describe your typical workday?

A: Typically, I start the day listening to a business news channel to be sure that I am up to date with any changes in the market and current news and events. I meet with clients regularly to discuss their financial goals (e.g., retirement, education planning), changes in their situation and the market, review their investments and track their progress. I also meet with prospective clients to learn about their goals and share how they may benefit by working with a financial advisor.

I also conduct financial planning—using tools to analyze clients' goals, running projections and illustrations, reviewing products and investments, and preparing strategies and recommendations. And throughout the day, I also implement the recommendations and transactions, such as creating investment accounts, insurance products, and placing trades.

Q: What do you like most about your job?

A: I love working with people. I've worked with many clients for over 20 years. It's so rewarding to see what our planning can accomplish—helping people achieve such goals as buying a new home, putting kids through college, and retiring. And being a source of comfort and support during sad and stressful times, such as a job loss or death in the family.

Q: What do you like least about your job?

A: Adapting to new and ever-changing technology. There is always a learning curve. But each new technology advancement brings value and eventually allows me to save time, research more, analyze deeper, and work more efficiently—so it's important to accept the changes and learn the advancements.

Fortunately, I no longer have to spend my time in areas that I like the least . . . but I certainly did early in my career. When I first started my career, I had to phone ("cold call") to schedule new appointments. That consisted of hours upon hours of phoning each week for a few years. Now I am fortunate to get referrals (word-of-mouth marketing).

Q: What personal qualities do you find most valuable for this type of work?

A: Trustworthiness and honesty. Finances and money are so important to people. To establish relationships with clients, they need to feel they can trust you and know you're putting their best interests first.

Being able to communicate. To be able to articulate strategies and recommendations. And more important, to listen. Every client is different, all with their own unique/specific goals and values.

Being analytical. Though technology and tools can help analyze and deliver advice, being able to understand the math behind investing, taxes, compound interest is so important.

Q: What advice do you have for students who might be interested in this career?

A: Keep learning. Read books, take business courses, talk to a mentor and your peers, listen to business news stations/podcasts—all will allow you to grow as a professional in your field. Also, consider an internship or shadowing or interviewing an advisor. Understand it will take time. . . . It can be a grind in your early years. Many hours, months, and years of learning, marketing, and building a practice. But if you enjoy it and stick with it, it is so rewarding.

Other Jobs If You Like Working with People

Administrative assistant
Career coach
Childcare worker
Community outreach coordinator
Concierge
Customer service representative
Education administrator
Firefighter
Flight attendant
Health care administrator
Human resources specialist
Librarian
Medical assistant
Mental health counselor
Nonprofit program manager
Occupational therapist
Physical therapist
Preschool teacher
Probation officer
Public relations specialist
Receptionist
Recruiter
Restaurant server
Sales representative
School counselor
Special education teacher
Speech–language pathologist
Teacher
Tour guide
Volunteer coordinator

Editor's note: The online *Occupational Outlook Handbook* of the US Department of Labor's Bureau of Labor Statistics is an excellent source of information on jobs in hundreds of career fields, including many of those listed here. The *Occupational Outlook Handbook* may be accessed online at www.bls.gov/ooh.

Index

Picture Credits

Cover: ljubaphoto/iStockphoto

10: LightField/Shutterstock
18: Frazao Studio Latine/iStockphoto
34: skynesher/iStockphoto
43: Nic Neufeld/Shutterstock
50: Krakenimages.com/Shutterstock

About the Author

Carla Mooney is the author of many books for young adults and children. She lives in Pittsburgh, Pennsylvania, with her husband and three children.